The Battle of

Northampton

1460

Rupert Matthews

Acknowledgements

Photos, illustrations and maps are by the author except:
Delapre Abbey, Brookie - Flooded battlefield, Brookie - Eleanor Cross, Brookie.
Drawings by Leanne Goodall and Darren Bennett.

Website - www.BretwaldaBooks.com
Twitter - @Bretwaldabooks
Facebook - Bretwalda Books
Blog - bretwaldabooks.blogspot.co.uk/

Bretwalda Books
Unit 8, Fir Tree Close, Epsom,
Surrey KT17 3LD
info@BretwaldaBooks.com
www.BretwaldaBooks.com
ISBN 978-1-909099-55-5

CONTENTS

INTRODUCTION

The Battle of Northampton was one of the first great battles of the Wars of the Roses, and it was a real turning point. For years the disputes between the causes of York and Lancaster had been played out in the political arena but when the Lancastrians turned to violence they surprised and shocked the Yorkists. But not for long.

The Duke of York fled into exile in Ireland with one son, while a second went to France and the others sought sanctuary. It proved to be only a temporary defeat. With his dashing, talented ally the Earl of Warwick, York contacted friends and supporters across England. Word spread that the Yorkists should get ready to support their leader for he was coming home in the summer of 1460.

In the event it was Warwick and York's son Edward, Earl of March, who reached England first. London welcomed them with open arms and men flocked to join their standard. But lurking in the Midlands was the Duke of Buckingham with King Henry VI and an army of prodigious strength.

Warwick marched north, confronting Buckingham just outside Northampton. The battle was fought to the south of the crossing over the River Nene, in the grounds of Delapre Abbey. The site is now a golf course and - bunkers apart - has not changed much over the years. The battle that followed was savage and murderous. Cannon were present in numbers for the first time in a battle fought on English soil, though the older weapons of bow, sword and lance predominated.

The Wars of the Roses would continue for years after Northampton, but the battle fought here set the tone and the pattern for what was to follow: treachery, ruthless violence, political subterfuge and barbaric slaughter dominated at Northampton and were to become savagely typical of the Wars of the Roses in the decades that followed as England was torn apart in a civil war of unparalleled viciousness.

This book seeks to explain why the Battle of Northampton was fought, how it was fought and what its results turned out to be. So read on and learn how history was made in Northampton.

CHAPTER 1
THE WARS OF THE ROSES

The vicious dynastic conflict known to us as the Wars of the Roses tore England apart between 1455 and 1497. Although there were prolonged periods of peace within the wars, this was a period of violence, bloodshed and lawlessness such as England had not seen since the reign of King Stephen in the 12th century.

Historians have sought to link the wars to various social trends within England, to underlying economic factors and to religion. However, there can be little doubt that the prime cause of all the trouble was King Henry VI. Not that this was really his fault. Henry was a weak and simple man who suffered bouts of mental incapacity that came and went with startling suddenness. He would sit down to dinner, fall into a trance and not recover his sense for hours, days or weeks on end. Nobody could predict when the next bout would strike nor how long it would last.

What was clear was that there were unscrupulous men and women close to Henry who were only too willing to take advantage of his weakness and bouts of insanity for their own purposes. Contemporaries pinned most of the blame on Henry's wife, Queen Margaret of Anjou. She was an easy target being both French and a woman, but that does not mean she was blameless. Margaret was undoubtedly a greedy and vengeful woman who found it as hard to forgive a wrong as to remember a favour. Margaret was aided and abetted by Edmund Beaufort, Duke of Somerset. This nobleman was clever, talented and deeply dishonest. Together these two set up a court that was dominated by those whom they could buy or subvert, or who were willing allies in the task of siphoning government funds into private pockets.

Richard Duke of York was a very different character. Even his friends did not claim he was particulary clever, but he was honest, diligent and brave. As the leader of English armies in France he had won some impressive victories until he was pushed aside by a jealous Somerset who promptly lost a string of battles

5

to the French. Moved to Ireland to oversee the royal estates and interests, York set up a government as honest and efficient as that in England was corrupt and inept. Inevitably people began to draw comparisons between York and Somerset.

What made the situation all the more dangerous was that King Henry VI was not, strictly speaking, the rightful king. Back in 1399 Richard II had been ousted from power by a popular uprising led by Henry of Bolingbroke, Duke of Lancaster. When Richard then conveniently died in prison, Henry became King Henry IV. He claimed the throne as he was the son of John of Gaunt, third son of King Edward III. However, John of Gaunt had had an elder brother named Lionel whose daughter Philippa had just died leaving a nine year old girl, Anne Mortimer, as her heiress. At the time nobody wanted a little girl as monarch, so Henry of Bolingbroke became Henry IV.

However young Anne had later married her cousin Richard of Conisburgh who was another grandson of Edward III. Their son was Richard, Duke of York. By strict rules of inheritance, York should have been king. As a young man York seemed perfectly happy with his lot as a senior and wealthy nobleman, but when Henry went mad he began to reconsider his claims to the throne. That, of course, made Margaret and Somerset all the more determined to get rid of him.

In 1453 Henry fell into a stupor more prolonged than before. A Council of Regency was set up with York as Lord Protector. He promptly put Somerset under house arrest and tasked Margaret with caring for her husband. For the next two years York set about trying to restore the finances of government. He carefully closed down the worst corruptions, threw out dishonest officials and got the finances back into profit. Where he failed was in dealing with the private feuding of his fellow powerful nobles. Under Henry's weak government several nobles had recruited private armies and set about settling old scores with their swords. York had the support of a dashing young nobleman and talented soldier, the Earl of Warwick, but even so he was quite unable to stop the bloodshed.

Then in 1455 Henry recovered his senses. The Council of Regency was disbanded and Margaret and Somerset put back into office. It was at this point that a famous incident is supposed to have taken place, though contemporary evidence for it is lacking. A large group of nobles was taking the air in the gardens of the Temple Church in the city of London during a court meeting when York entered through one gate and Somerset a few seconds later by way of another. York then picked a white rose from a bush in the garden, the white rose being a heraldic badge associated with his family. Somerset promptly picked a red rose

6

from a different bush. Warwick then picked a white rose, followed by nobles supporting York, while those backing Somerset hurried to pick red roses and those unwilling to commit themselves in so obviously a dangerous dispute rushed to get out of the garden.

Whatever the truth of the events in the Temple Gardens, York retired to his estates, but Margaret would not let him be. She began putting together an alliance of nobles with grudges against York and Warwick, then sounded out lawyers as to grounds to charge York with treason.

York was alarmed, mustered a force of armed men and marched on London. At St Albans on 22 May 1455 York and Warwick met Somerset with his own

King Henry VI reigned from 1422 when he inherited the throne at the age of just nine months. He grew up to be a weak, indecisive man who suffered episodes of mental illness. His inability to keep a firm grip on government led to the Wars of the Roses.

A Victorian view of the incident in the Temple Garden, London, when nobles picked roses to indicate which side they supported in the dispute between York and Lancaster.

armed men. A short, brutal fight developed in which Somerset was killed. It was the first of the battles of the Wars of the Roses, but it was far from the last. Henry then fell into another coma and York again became Protector. He tried to be conciliatory, allowing the widowed Duchess of Somerset a generous pension as well as allowing the new Duke of Somerset to inherit his father's lands. York and

8

A contemporary view of the wedding of Henry VI and Margaret of Anjou. The wedding seemed to make perfect dynastic sense at the time, but would later lead to much trouble in the internal politics of England. Despite appearances, Margaret was not pregnant at the time of the wedding, her dress is merely fashionable for the date.

Warwick paid for a chantry chapel to be built in London where a priest said prayers daily for the souls of those killed at St Albans. These efforts at reconciliation culminated in the so-called "Love Day", a service of reconciliation held in St Paul's Cathedral, London, on Lady Day, 25 March, 1458.

Margaret of Anjou was not to be placated. She wanted revenge on York and power over England in her own hands. She spent months recruiting allies, bribing officials and spreading lies. She finally went public in April 1459 summoning an army to gather at Leicester on 10 May and demanding the arrest of York and Warwick. York tried to gather his own army, and won a preliminary skirmish at Bore Heath, but he was obviously outnumbered. York fled to Ireland with his second son, Edmund Earl of Rutland, while Warwick went to Calais (then part of England) with York's second son Edward Earl of March.

Warwick and York spent the winter sounding out nobles and others, gathering support and laying their plans. Among those they found willing to listen was Francesco dei Coppini, the Papal Legate to England. Coppini had been sent to England by Pope Pius II seeking men or money to support a war against the Moslem Turks. Margaret of Anjou had treated him rudely and with contempt, making him an easy target for Warwick's gentle talents of charm.

On 25 June 1460 Warwick and Edward of March landed at Sandwich with a small army. They marched to Canterbury where they met Coppini and together said prayers at the shrine of St Thomas a Becket. This was a crucial symbolic act. Thomas had been very popular with the poorer people due to his many acts of charity, but had been killed by knights loyal to King Henry II after getting into a dispute with Henry over the rights of the Church. By bending their knees at the shrine, Edward and Warwick were indicating that they were on the side of the poor and the Church.

They then moved on to London, where on 2 July the citizens threw open the gates of the city. The merchants of the city had respected York and welcomed the order and honest government he had brought, while they idolised the dashing Warwick. Supporters of York from across southern England had been alerted and now came marching into London to swell the ranks of the army. The City of London voted a loan of £1,000 to the Duke of York "for the peace and prosperity of the king and kingdom". Next day the Duke of Norfolk came in to join Warwick, only one of many noblemen bringing men to join the Yorkist cause.

By chance there was also in London Thomas Bouchier, Archbishop of Canterbury, who was presiding over a convocation of English bishops. The bishops were, understandably, nervous of the sudden arrival of thousands of armed men. Bouchier came from the highest ranks of the nobility, being a half brother to the Duke of Buckingham, a brother to the Earl of Essex and a cousin to the Earl of Gloucester. He was not overawed by the nobles, and summoned Warwick and Edward to appear before him at Lambeth Palace. What, Bouchier demanded to know, were they up to.

Warwick and Edward told Bouchier that they had come to rescue King Henry from evil advisers and to restore good, honest government to the kingdom under the guidance of the Duke of York. Bouchier, it would seem, was unconvinced. After all the two noblemen had brought thousands of men with them from Calais and hundreds more were streaming into London every day. In front of the assembled bishops Bouchier produced the Canterbury Cross, a holy relic of enormous power and significance. He made Warwick and Edward lay their hands on the cross and swear on their honour that they neither intended nor would do any harm to King Henry. Both swore willingly.

This was, for a medieval noble, an important and significant step. It was firmly believed that God watched over holy relics. An oath taken on such a relic was binding not only in honour but also in religion. If such an oath were broken, the oathbreaker would be condemned by God to Hell, or at least to Purgatory, and would lose all respect in the eyes of their fellow humans. That Warwick and Edward took such a plainly worded oath so wilingly convinced Bouchier and the other bishops that whatever else the two men might be up to, killing Henry was not on their agenda.

Bouchier agreed to accompany the Yorkist army, along with several other bishops, and to use his position to try to broker a deal between the two sides when they met. Warwick seemed enthusiastic about this idea. He said that all he wanted to do was to meet the king face to face without the evil advisers being present so that he could talk to the king and convince him of the need for honest government. Whether Bouchier actually believed this or not is unclear, but certainly he was convinced that the Yorkists meant no harm to the king.

Margaret had known that the Yorkists would return. She was in Cheshire with her son Edward Prince of Wales raising troops to oppose York when he landed from Ireland. Henry VI was in the Midlands with Humphrey Stafford, Duke of Buckingham. There they too were raising men, having been warned in advance that London would declare for York.

On hearing that Warwick and Edward were in London, Buckingham moved his own army to Northampton. The town lay between the two main routes north from London, the Great North Road to York and Watling Street to Wroxeter and Cheshire. The town also lay between London and Warwick's estates, blocking off a major source of recruitment. Having reached Northampton, Buckingham dug in and waited.

11

CHAPTER 2
LEADERS AT NORTHAMPTON

The Lancastrian forces at Northampton were nominally under the command of King Henry VI. Henry had been born the son of King Henry V in 1421, which made him 39 at the time of the battle. He was only nine months old when he inherited the crown of England from his father. He grew up to be a kindly and devout man, but his childish nature and simple mind made him a weak king. Henry slipped into periodic bouts of insanity which made his grip on government even less secure.

Henry was no more fit to lead an army than to rule a kingdom, so real command fell to Humphrey Stafford Duke of Buckingham, the most experienced diplomat and commander at the battle. Born in 1402, Buckingham was 58 when he drew up his men outside Northampton. Through his mother, Buckingham was a great grandson of King Edward III, yet another royal relative active in the Wars of the Roses. His father had died when he was barely a year old, leaving him the title of Earl of Stafford and a handsome income of £1260 a year, not bad when the average worker would get a penny a day. He was knighted in 1421 and became a Privy Councillor to the infant Henry VI in 1424. In 1430 he went to Normandy to take part in the fighting against the French and although he did not have an independent command, he did gain valuable experience of the business of war.

When his mother died in 1438 he inherited her lands, tripling his income at a stroke, and the title of Earl of Buckingham. He was now one of the richest and most noble men in England. As such he was made a Knight of the Garter and entrusted with a string of diplomatic missions. His military experience was broadened by being made Captain of Calais, effectively commander of the English forces in northern France, as well as Warden of the Cinque Ports (a naval command) and Constable of Dover Castle.

When the disputes between Somerset and York broke out in earnest, Buckingham played the role of peace-keeper between his two truculent cousins. By way of family links, Buckingham had a foot in both camps. His daughter was

Richard Neville, 16th Earl of Warwick, as shown in the Rous Roll. This document was drawn up by John Rous in about 1483 and is a major source for history of the period of the Wars of the Roses. Rous presents a highly biased pro-Yorkist view of the wars. In 1460 Warwick was one of the richest and most influential noblemen in England, though many older noblemen regarded him as something of an upstart.

married to Somerset's son while he himself was married to a cousin of Warwick. Buckingham declared himself to be a firm supporter of Henry VI, and sought constantly to push for good government and impartial justice. He quarrelled constantly with Somerset, but refused to accept the more radical solutions of York.

At the Battle of St Albans in 1455 he had commanded King Henry's bodyguard. He was slightly wounded and captured by the Earl of Warwick. Buckingham continued to try to find common ground between the two sides, expressing shock that the dispute had come to blows and seeking to bring people to their senses. Finally realising that Margaret and York were unwilling to find any sort of compromise deal, Buckingham decided to remain loyal to King Henry, even though that meant siding with Margaret.

In October 1459 he led a Lancastrian army to Ludford Bridge in Shropshire, where his friendship with several of the lesser nobles in York's army persuaded them to change sides or slip away in the night. As a result Buckingham was able to drive York into exile in France almost without striking a blow. He took the Duchess of York and her three youngest children into his own care, being careful not to pass them on to the vengeful Queen Margaret. Henry VI rewarded Buckingham with estates confiscated from those who had gone into exile with York. He was in London through the winter of 1459-60 trying to muster men and money for the cause of King Henry, but finding his efforts largely thwarted by the unpopularity of Queen Margaret. He had nevertheless mustered a reasonably large army by the standards of the day, and marched it north away from pro-York

Edward Earl of March was nominally second in command of the Yorkist army at the Battle of Northampton. At the time, however, he was only 18 years old and had never fought in a battle. Many historians believe that it was the experienced Lord Fauconberg who was the real commander.

London two or three weeks before Warwick and Edward Earl of March got to the city.

Serving under Buckingham was Lord Edmund Grey of Ruthin. By his family links Grey was firmly linked to the Lancastrian cause. By his mother he was a great grandson of John of Gaunt, Duke of Lancaster, and therefore a cousin to Henry VI. He married Lady Katherine Percy, daughter of Henry Percy, Earl of Northumberland. The Percys had a long running feud with the Nevilles, the family of the Earl of Warwick. However, Grey had got involved in a bitter dispute with Henry Holland, Duke of Exeter and a key supporter of Queen Margaret. Exeter was bad tempered and particularly rapacious when it came to exploiting contacts at court for his own benefit. Exeter had made a bid to seize control of the wealthy manor of Ampthill, Bedfordshire, from Grey on rather dubious grounds and was busily using bribery and pressure to get his way. Nevertheless, Grey had remained a staunch supporter of Buckingham in his efforts to find a compromise peace and to be loyal to the anointed King, Henry VI, come what may.

Grey, like Buckingham, had seen extensive service in the French wars. He had fought in the Aquitaine campaigns of 1438-40 and been knighted as a consequence. He sat on the Council of Regency from 1456 to 1458 and was notable for his refusal to get dragged into supporting either York or Queen Margaret. At the time of the Battle of Northampton he was 44 years old.

Leading the advancing Yorkist army was Richard Neville, Earl of Warwick. Although the title of Earl of Warwick was one of the oldest and most prestigious in the English nobility, Richard Neville was himself something of a newcomer. He gained the title through his wife, Anne Beauchamp, who herself gained the title only after her elder siblings died without heirs. Warwick's father's family had come from the gentry of County Durham and had first gained a title only in 1397. Warwick was, therefore, viewed as something of a nouveau riche by the more established noble families. There was, however, no doubting Warwick's good looks, intelligence nor his abilities.

Warwick's military experience began in 1448 when he served in the war against Scotland. He campaigned around the border for more than a year, then stayed in the area to help supervise the construction of defences and an efficient scouting system to watch for future incursions. It was soon after the Scottish war that the Duke of Somerset launched a legal action against Warwick. The dispute centred on lands that Anne Beauchamp had been left by her father, but which Somerset contended should have passed to a different branch of the Beauchamp family -

and so to his own wife. Somerset soon began to use his influence with Henry VI to get his way in court. It was this dispute that convinced Warwick that Somerset and Margaret were deeply corrupt and had to be ousted from government.

In 1455 Warwick had masterminded the victory for York at St Albans. In thanks York made Warwick Constable of Calais. At the time Calais belonged to England. It was an important city for all English wool exported to the continent went through Calais, where it could be assessed and taxed. The command also brought with it control of all English troops in northern France, the largest standing army under the English crown.

In this post Warwick was involved in campaigns and skirmishes against both the French and the Burgundians. Although these campaigns were all fairly minor, Warwick showed that he knew how to supply an army, pay the men and keep morale high. He also gained a reputation for being able to come up with daring and innovative ideas that kept his opponents constantly on their toes and more than once caught them by surprise.

Warwick proved to be popular in Calais with both the merchants and the soldiers. When he fled into exile with Edward, Earl of March, it was to Calais that he went. And it was in Calais that he put together his army with which to invade England. He thus came to Northampton as a younger, less experienced commander than his opponents, but one with a growing reputation. He was 32 years old.

Alongside Warwick, and very much in his shadow, was the 18 year old Edward, Earl of March. Edward was the eldest son of Richard, Duke of York, and thus by Yorkist reckoning had more right to the throne than did Henry VI. He was tall, broad-shouldered and extremely good looking. Young Edward already had a reputation with the women, one that would only grow as the years passed.

Like all noblemen of his time he had trained for war from childhood and had been instructed in the skills needed to run and organise large landed estates. Rather more unusually, he had also interested himself in the new and growing business of trade. His opponents whispered that Edward was more interested in the merchants' wives and daughters than in their trade, but his interest in how merchants made money seems to have been genuine enough. In later life he would show himself to have a deep understanding of how trade operated and how merchants and their wealth could be used to good effect.

Edward's military experience was almost non-existent. He had taken part in the abortive campaign that ended in humiliation at Ludford Bridge in 1459 and had spent the winter watching Warwick recruit an army in Calais, but he had seen no fighting.

Older and vastly more experienced than either Warwick or Edward was William Neville, Lord Fauconberg, who led the advance guard of the Yorkist army. Some historians suspect that Fauconberg was the real Yorkist commander at Northampton, only the later fame of Warwick and Edward putting his role into the shade. He was the uncle Warwick and, like him, had gained his title and much of his money by marrying an heiress. Aged 55 at the time of the battle, Fauconberg had been a soldier for most of the previous 34 years.

Fauconberg's military career had begun in 1426 on the Scottish borders, operating from his own estates in north Yorkshire. In 1436 Fauconberg went to France where he served under the Duke of York. He seems to have admired York's abilities very much, but like many others did not care for York personally. Over the following years Fauconberg fought a series of successful actions against the French, gaining particular fame for the capture of the port of Harfleur in 1441. In 1449 he was ambushed by the French when he had only a small escort. He fought bravely and even when all was lost carried on defending himself. When wounded and down he still refused to surrender, declaring he was an English nobleman and would not surrender to any French peasant. Only the fortuitous arrival of a French knight both saved his life and secured his surrender.

In 1453 Fauconberg was released by the French after his wife paid a hefty ransom. He then returned to the Scottish border where he origanised patrols and defences, though there was no fighting. In 1455 he was with King Henry at St Albans, but almost immediately changed sides to support his old commander the Duke of York, to whom he thereafter remained loyal. When York made Warwick Constable of Calais, he appointed Fauconberg his deputy. It has long been suspected that York put Fauconberg in Calais to keep an experienced eye on the dashing, but rash Warwick. It is likewise thought that Fauconberg may have been the real commander at Northampton, at least so far as York was concerned. What Warwick thought of this is unknown.

CHAPTER 3
MEN, WEAPONS AND TACTICS

The armies of the Wars of the Roses were raised in three basic ways. First there were the town and county militias, second were the retainers of the various noblemen and third were mercenaries, mostly foreigners. The size of the armies involved has provoked a lot of dispute. Contemporary chroniclers had not, by and large, been anywhere near the fighting since most of them were monks or clerics. They recorded figures of anything between 20,000 and 80,000 men for the armies involved, but this was probably based more on guesswork than anything else. Modern historians have tended to reduce these numbers substantially, suggesting that most armies were around 10,000 to 15,000 strong with the largest army fielded at this date being the 35,000 Lancastrians who fought at Towton in 1461. However, it must be said that these historians are working on little more than guesswork either. The only firm information we have comes in scraps here and there, such as the fact that in 1454 the Duke of Buckingham paid for 2,000 badges to be sewn on the cloaks of his men going to patrol the Scottish Border or that in 1455 Coventry town council bought 100 suits of clothes for the citizens who were serving in the militia that year. It is likely that in the earlier phases of the war the armies were larger than later on, though what the number at any particular battle may have been it is impossible to know for certain.

The town and county militias in the 15th century were the descendants of the old feudal levy. This had stated that every able-bodied man aged 16 to 60 had to be ready to defend his local town or county in times of war. The first 40 days was unpaid and compulsory, but after that the men had to be paid and had to volunteer to serve. It had been so long since England had been invaded by anyone that the original system had fallen into disuse. Instead it had evolved into a way of raising a semi-professional force of men for longer periods of time.

Each town and city was expected to have a full time guard which patrolled the city walls, secured the city gates at night and kept order on the streets. The men would also guard the gates during the day, collecting any tolls that were due from merchants and keeping an eye open for undesirables. These men might number only a dozen or so and were employed full time by the council, their equipment, food and lodging usually being provided.

There was also the militia, sometimes termed "trained bands", made up of citizens who were trained to use weapons at weekends, but who worked at their own trades during the week. Arrangements varied, but these men were usually paid a small amount each month in return for turning up to train equipped with weapons and armour. Each town or county employed a Constable who was responsible for training the men, checking their equipment and recording any absences from training sessions. In times of war he was the commander of the unit on campaign.

When a royal "commission of array" arrived asking for the militia to turn out it usually specified the numbers of men needed and how long they would serve

This hobilar, or pricker, is typical of Wars of the Roses cavalry. He wears a helmet of metal padded with wool. His leather sleeveless jack has overlapping metal plates and is worn over a mail shirt that reaches to the elbows and to mid-thigh. His leg armour is made of plate and covers him from upper thigh to toe. For weapons he has a long but light lance, backed by a sword. Such men had many uses on campaign, but few on the battlefield.

19

for. It was then the task of the local authorities to find the men, usually volunteers from among those who came for training. While the men were usually expected to provide their own weapons and armour, it was the town council or county sheriff who paid and supplied their clothes and food out of local taxation. In most instances the men would be provided with a new suit of clothes and a travelling cloak before they set off. These clothes were provided in bulk by the authorities and while they fell short of being a uniform they did tend to be in a uniform colour or pattern which meant that all men from one town or county were dressed alike. Nottingham, for instance, is known to have supplied red outfits while Coventry favoured red and green stripes.

As for weapons, it would seem that the militia tended to go for weapons that did not demand much in the way of skill to wield in battle. In 1457 the men of Bridport, Dorset, paraded armed with a sword and dagger each, plus a shield, helmet and quilted jacket. The rural village of Ewelme in Oxfordshire provided a rather more mixed array. Among the 6 men recorded as parading for training were two archers, one of whom had a helmet and body armour, three men with partial armour and a bill and one man who had no armour and was armed with "a staff". Quite how much use the last would be in battle is unclear, though all armies needed someone to collect firewood and dig latrines so perhaps that was his task.

In normal conditions these militia did little fighting for they were not destined for overseas service in the French wars. Instead they were used for duties closer to home, manning coastal defences, castles and assorted strongpoints. But the years of the Wars of the Roses were not usual conditions.

The militia were under the control of the crown and so were expected to be loyal to the reigning monarch. This was part of the military set up that for centuries had made England far less prone to rebellions and civil wars than other European states. With so much of the military apparatus in the hands of the monarch, it was a brave nobleman indeed who started an armed rebellion.

However, the Duke of York was not launching an armed rebellion against the king. He always made it very clear that he was loyal to King Henry VI, but was instead seeking to free the king from dishonest advisers. He therefore felt free to summon militias in the name of the king, as did Queen Margaret. This put the local authorities in something of a quandary. If they ignored a commission of array they might be charged with treason, while if they answered it they might be aiding a cause they did not support. Few records have survived to show how local authorities coped, but we know of the reaction of Norwich in 1461.

In the spring the city received a commission of array from Queen Margaret in the name of King Henry VI. The commission demanded 120 fully equiped infantry to fight against rebels and traitors. Norwich city council complied promptly enough, getting volunteers together, providing them with campaigning suits of clothes and checking over their arms and armour. But before the 120 men set off they held a meeting in front of the cathedral. After some discussion the men decided that they favoured the Yorkist cause, and so marched to fight against Margaret instead of for her. The council was, apparently, not consulted and the decision made by the men themselves.

We know that militias fought on both sides during the Wars of the Roses, but unlike the men of Norwich in 1461 we do not know how they decided which side to support.

If details of the militia are rather scarce, we know rather more about the retainers as this system involved cash changing hands for written contracts, called indentures, some of which have survived. The system began to develop under Edward III who needed a reliable supply of men willing to serve across the Channel in France.

By the time of Edward III in the mid-14th century the old feudal system had more or less broken down. Instead of knights and barons who held land from the crown paying for it by serving as an armed man when needed, it had become

This handgunner is based on an English manuscript dating to about 1470. His gun is an iron tube closed at one end. Gunpowder and bullet were rammed down the open end and fired by inserting a hot wire into a hole at the closed end. He wears a mail shirt reaching almost to elbows and knees. Over this is a short-sleeved shirt of padded wool. His open faced helmet is of iron, probably padded with wool. His knees are protected by iron plates, but his legs and lower arms are otherwise unprotected. He has a sword for use at close quarters once he has fired his gun.

21

more normal for them to pay a tax known as scutage. This was, in theory, set at a rate that allowed the monarch to hire a mercenary to do the military service instead. However, Edward had found that foreign mercenaries were unreliable. Instead he gradually developed the indenture system.

Under this system the king gave a noble or knight a contract to provide a set number of armed men of various types for a specific period of time for a set rate of pay. The contracts generally ran for three months, six months or a year. Most were concerned with the summer campaigning season, while the annual contracts were for castle guard duty and patrolling frontiers. Because the indentures were usually renewed year after year, the men became effectively full time professional soldiers. Knowing that they would get paid for years, the men realised it was worth their while to invest in top quality equipment and put in the many hours of training needed to master the often complex skills of medieval warfare.

Rates of pay varied, but the average for the mid 15th century was for an archer to get three pennies a day, a hobilar six pennies, a man at arms one shilling, a knight two shillings a knight banneret four shillings and a nobleman six shillings and eight pennies. There was usually a "regard" paid at the end of the contract, assuming that the men had performed their duties well. This might be as much as the value of the contract, but was usually less. All pay was in cash and if the pay fell into arrears the men were entitled to go home before the contract ended.

The ratios between the different types of man also varied, but by 1450 it was usual for there to be five or six archers for each man at arms, three or four men at arms for each knight (nobles counting as knights for this purpose). The size of indentures varied wildly with individual knights agreeing a contract to come along in person along with half a dozen archers, while the famous commanders might agree to provide up to 4,000 men. Interestingly the numbers of men a commander could put together bore no relation to his social rank. The Earl of Devon could muster only 110 men, while Sir Robert Knollys, a mere knight, could regularly field over 3,000 men. It was fame and competence that enabled a man to attract followers, not wealth or rank.

As a rule the same men served under the same commander year after year. This produced a strong sense of team spirit or cohesion within the English armies from around 1360 onwards that other European armies simply failed to match. Foreign chroniclers recorded again and again that English armies were basically just that - English. They were not the feudal levies raised by great lords from their peasants. This was to have a profound impact on English society as noblemen and knights came to see themselves as national team leaders with close links to the men who served them, be it in arms or as tenant farmers. In return the soldiers and peasants viewed the nobles as their local leaders and champions, turning to the local noble when in difficulty or needing help of some kind. On the continent, by contrast, nobles came to see themselves as part of a social caste that had closer links to the nobles of other countries than to the peasants of their own. The peasants reciprocated by viewing the nobles as remote and unhelpful figures. The social trends were slow to develop, but were all the stronger for that. In later centuries the differences would help explain why Europe erupted into revolutions, while Britain did not.

While some indentures were between knights and nobles, the majority were with the king directly. Even those that were between subjects were for moneys that originated with the king, and could be withheld by him. As with the militia system it was a system that was designed to provide the king with a near

Most armoured infantry during the Wars of the Roses were armed something like this figure. He wears an iron helmet and full upper harness composed of breastplate with groin plates over a mail shirt. His lower arms and hands are protected by plate armour gauntlets. His legs are quite unprotected. His main weapon is a bill, a weapon on a shaft over six feet long that combined a thrusting point with a chopping blade and sometimes, as here, a back hook to pull enemies to the ground. The bill was based on a farmer's hedging tool and was a distinctively English weapon. He has a sword to use in case his bill breaks or for close infighting.

monopoly of armed might. However, the individual commanders did enjoy a degree of freedom. They could choose not to serve one year, for example, if the deal on offer was not to their liking.

In the context of the Wars of the Roses, the fact that the provision of armed men was in the hands of nobles and knights has been used by some historians to suggest that armies could be raised quickly for anyone who could pay. Things were not that simple, however. By the 1450s English soldiers were habitually loyal to the crown. A commander who sought to recruit his usual men to fight against the king might, and sometimes did, find himself unable to recruit anyone.

Again it was York's claim to be raising men to rescue King Henry VI from his evil advisers that proved crucial. Nearly everyone knew that the administration of the kingdom was in a dire state and so could accept that serving the Yorkist cause was not rebellion, but true loyalty. Not everyone agreed, of course, and many remained loyal to Henry even though they despised Margaret and her cronies.

The most numerous mercenaries in English armies serving in France had been Welsh. At this date Wales had ceased to be an independent country, or rather a

This archer is typical of the period. Because large numbers of archers served on both sides he is wearing fairly substantial armour to provide protection against incoming arrows. He has a mail shirt reaching to elbows and knees. Over this he wears a sleeveless jack made of up to 22 layers of linen over which are stitched plates of iron or horn. His sallet-style helmet is of steel, padded with wool. His lower arms are free to allow him to draw his bow. The lower legs are unarmoured, probably to allow him to move nimbly around the battlefield. His bow is the standard longbow of the period and he has a quiver of arrows at his belt. His sword and buckler are for hand to hand fighting.

collection of them, but had not yet been fully integrated into the English systems of government. The Welsh did not, therefore, provide militias or indentured retinues. Instead they provided companies of men recruited directly by royal officials.

A typical Welsh company consisted of 100 men, four cooks, one translator (few Welshmen spoke English), one standard bearer, one crier (a man with a loud voice to shout out commands) one physician and a commander. Most of the men were archers, but about a quarter were men armed with spears or poleaxes whose task was to protect the archers from cavalry or other attack.

Irishmen were also hired as mercenaries. They tended to be lightly armed men mounted on small ponies. Few of these Irish horsemen were armoured, other than a helmet, with only the leaders having mail coats or plate breastplates. For weaponry the Irish carried two or three light javelins, plus a sword or long knife.

On campaign in France, the Irish horsemen were used to scout ahead and to the flanks of the army. They could fight skirmishes with small numbers of French, capture peasants for questioning and forage for food, but were not much use in battle against the French.

The Scots and French were never hired as mercenaries as they were regarded

This fully armoured knight wears the very latest and finest armour, so he must be a rich man. The body is entirely encased in plates of quality steel shaped to fit the individual. Pieces of mail are used to give added protection at joints. His main weapon is a poleaxe, with a long sword as a secondary weapon. This sort of armour was surprisingly light and flexible, allowing the wearer freedom of movement.

as the national enemies of England, but other foreigners were hired in numbers. Most of these men came from Germany or the Low Countries. They had contracts not too dissimilar to the indentures that recruited English soldiers. The men were recruited by a local knight or lord, who then agreed a deal with his employer. While the English had scruples about fighting their monarch, the foreign mercenaries had no such issues. They would cheerfully fight for whoever paid them.

The majority of mercenaries serving in the Wars of the Roses were specialists. Typical were the handgunners and petardiers. Handgunners were equipped with guns that consisted of a tube of iron, open at one end. The gunpowder and lead pellet were pushed down from the open end with a rammer. A hot iron wire or burning coal was then thrust into a small hole at the closed end which set off the charge and propelled the lead pellet out the other end. These early hand guns produced a huge amount of smoke and noise, which could serve to frighten horses and unsettle inexperienced troops, but their actual effectiveness as weapons is unclear. They seem to have had a range not much short of the longbow, but their rate of fire was much slower - about one shot every minute or so compared to a longbow shooting ten arrows a minute. At close range they were more effective for the heavy lead pellet could pass straight through one man to kill or wound the man behind, something an arrow could not do.

Petardiers were equipped with petards, clay pots about five inches across that were filled with gunpowder and scraps of old iron or pottery. A fuse entered the petard and was lit before the pot was thrown at the enemy. The range of a petard was obviously limited, but again at close quarters they could be horrific weapons. A petard exploding among a densely packed formation of infantry could kill or wound many men, opening up a gap in the formation that could prove fatal if it were quickly filled.

Because these men had no scruples, all the senior noblemen engaged in the Wars of the Roses hired them in numbers. In 1461 the Earl of Warwick hired 500 handgunners from Burgundy for the summer and in 1485 Henry Tudor had over a thousand.

Artillery were also to be seen on battlefields during the Wars of the Roses, manned by either foreign mercenaries or English gunners. The really big cannon, bombards able to hurl stones weighing 200lb, were not seen on battlefields. They were massively expensive to make, difficult to transport and virtually immobile on the battlefield. Essential in sieges, they were simply too big and heavy for

A standard infantry formation from the Wars of the Roses. The armoured billmen and men at arms are formed up four ranks deep in the centre while the archers are pushed forward on the flanks to shoot at the advancing enemy. The commanding knight and his assistants stand behind to direct movement.

battles. Battlefield artillery went by a variety of names, though culverine and serpentine seem to have been popular. These guns had barrels about eight to 12 feet long and fired stone or iron shot weighing about 10 to 20lb. The cannon were mounted on carriages that had two large wheels and a long wooden trail behind. The trail was used to pull the gun around the battlefield, or swivel it from side to side before firing. The barrel could be raised or lowered with a wooden wedge to alter the range. On the move the trail was fixed to a cart containing the ammunition and pulled by oxen or horses. There was usually at least one other cart filled with ammunition.

What all these guns and firearms had in common was their complete unpredictability. Even in the hands of a trained and experienced gunner, the weapons would behave completely differently one day to how they did the next. The problem was the gunpowder.

At this date making gunpowder was more of an art that a science. Nobody understood the chemical reactions involved, so getting the mix right was down to trial and error, with each gunner fiercely guarding his own preferred method. Of the three ingredients, charcoal was by far the cheapest and easiest to source. Sulphur was more expensive, but again not too difficult to come by. It was saltpetre that really represented the problem.

Saltpetre, as its name meaning "salt-rock" suggests could be mined, but only in a very few places. Most countries resorted to manufacturing saltpetre. This was a messy and protracted business that involved collecting together large quantities of horse, cattle or sheep manure, mixing it with wood ash and piling it up inside a wooden barn which had a waterproof floor of rammed clay. The organic mass was then wetted thoroughly each week with human urine for a year. Then the wetting was stopped and the barn sealed shut to allow the rotting mass to dry out gradually. As the water evaporated slowly from the surface of the putrid mess, it brought to the surface raw saltpetre which precipitated out as white crystals. Each cubic yard of manure produced about 16lb of saltpetre.

The saltpetre produced by this method was a mix of various organic nitrates, the composition of which varied with the quality of the raw materials, the temperatures at which it rotted and the time allowed for drying. Each batch of saltpetre had its own qualities that affected the performance of the gunpowder that it was used to make. Very often the crucial feature of this crude saltpetre proved to be its hydrostatic properties. All saltpetre will absorb water from the air if left uncovered, but certain forms of raw saltpetre will absorb it more quickly than others. On damp days the saltpetre will suck up moisture faster than ever. And damp saltpetre meant gunpowder that did not explode very well.

Gunpowder in the 15th century was a simple mix of charcoal, sulphur and saltpetre for as yet no way had been found of combining the three into a stable powder. Each of these three has a quite different density, so if a barrel of mixed gunpowder was put onto a cart and trundled over the bumpy roads of the period for any amount of time the three components would separate out. Before a barrel of gunpowder could be used it had to be tumbled around the ground for quite some time to remix the ingredients. It was more usual, therefore, for the ingredients to be transported separately and for the gunpowder to be mixed only when it was needed.

The gunpowder then had to "proved" before it could be used. This generally involved putting a measured quantity of powder into a handgun and ramming down a lead pellet of known weight. The gun was then fired, with the gunner watching carefully to gauge the force and sound of the explosion, as well as the distance the shot was carried. From this the gunner could then work out how much powder should be used to produce a standard explosive force. The powder would then be parceled up into separate cloth bags accordingly.

Fieldworks such as those used at Northampton were a feature of several battles at this period. They could be dug quickly and gave substantial protection against assault for defending troops. The ditch and bank has a wooden wall that is thick enough to be proof against arrows.

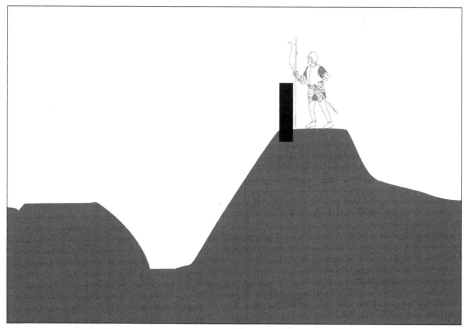

As can be imagined, getting guns ready to fire was a laborious, lengthy and highly skilled business. Even then things did not always go right. As recently as 1460 King James II of Scotland was to be killed when a cannon burst as he fired it.

For centuries the battlefield had been ruled by the armoured knight on horseback. A well timed charge by heavy horsemen had been able to smash enemy formations and win a battle with ease. From 1346 onwards, however, the English had rendered this tactic obsolete with a novel tactical formation. The English put their armoured men on foot, drawn up in a line between four and eight ranks deep. The men stood shoulder to shoulder to form a solid block of men. A high proportion of these men were armed with pole weapons of one sort or another. At first these were mostly spears, but by the time of the Wars of the Roses these had mostly been replaced by bills. Horses will not run headlong into a solid barrier, be it a brick wall or a mass of men. So long as the men on foot stood their ground, charging cavalry would come to a halt. The horsemen would then be vulnerable to the pole weapons of the infantry.

Standing on the flanks of the densely packed armoured infantry were bodies of archers. What made archery so effective was the fact that the archers were using a tactic that became known as the arrowstorm. Instead of the archers being dispersed among the arrayed infantry they were grouped together as solid groups of archers. This enabled them for the first time to come under the command of an experienced knight whose sole task was to direct the archery. A group of archers could be ordered to shoot at the same time at the same target.

What made the arrowstorm effective was a realisation that the archers did not actually need to aim to hit a particular man, nor even a group of men. Such a feat was beyond most archers at ranges over 100 yards. Instead all the archers needed to do was to shoot in the given direction at a given range. Even the most average archer could put an arrow to within 20 yards or so of a chosen spot at 200 yards range.

A single archer making such a shot would have little impact, but by grouping the archers together in numbers and making them all shoot at once the situation was transformed. A force of 200 archers would put 200 arrows simultaneously down into a designated area. The scattering of arrows by mediocre aiming would matter little, and indeed would help ensure that the arrows hit something.

The lack of a need for precision aiming speeded up the business of shooting. Instead of it taking up to 20 seconds to knock an arrow, choose a target, draw and shoot, archers could now knock, point in the right direction and let fly in just 10 seconds. If arrows were put point downward in the turf in front of the archer instead of being kept in the quiver, the shooting time per arrow was down to 6 seconds. It became usual for each archer to put about six arrows in front of him preparatory to shooting.

The combined results of these changes was awesome. The archery commander would watch the developing battle and select an enemy formation to be the target for his men. When the enemy came within range, the commander would point out the direction and call a range. The archers would then begin shooting, each man letting fly six arrows in 24 seconds or so.

The deployment of handgunners is not fully understood. One possible explanation has them forming much of the front rank of an infantry formation surrounded by armoured infantry. The knightly commander of the unit stands behind to shout orders.

At the receiving end the result was a veritable storm of arrows. Contemporary writers, awed by the sight, compared the arrows to falling hail or rain. A force of 500 archers could put 2400 arrows into an area of battlefield measuring 40 metres square with ease. Such a concentration of missiles in such a small space would guarantee that any man or horse in that patch of ground would be almost guaranteed to be hit by at least one arrow. No wonder contemporaries were so awed.

There would then follow a short pause while the archers got more arrows from their quivers and pushed them into the ground in front of them. The commander would use this time to assess the damage inflicted on the enemy, scan the battlefield for the next most urgent target and decide whom to shoot at next. Again the commander would point and call out a range, again the arrowstorm would be let fly. Of course, such tactics were enormously costly in terms of arrows, and arrows were not cheap. Only kings or the richest nobles could afford to supply large numbers of archers. It was reckoned that each archer needed 400 arrows for a campaign, and with each arrow costing a penny that was expensive.

By the Wars of the Roses the arrowstorm had become slightly less decisive. Knights usually fought on foot and new types of armour had been invented. This new armour took the form of steel plates shaped to wrap around the body. The plate armour was also designed to have smooth shapes and flowing profiles so that an arrow would glance off it more easily. Even so the new armour was not entirely proof against arrows. Given the huge numbers of arrows shot during battles at this period some at least would find a weak spot and penetrate to the man's flesh. Even if that did not happen the sheer force of an arrow strike was considerable. An arrow had more than enough momentum to knock a man over, or to daze him badly if it hit his helmet. Moreover many men could not afford such very expensive armour and so went into battle only partially armoured, or wearing old fashioned mail that was less proof against arrows.

Nevertheless the usual battlefield tactic at this date was still to deploy knights and men at arms in a solid phalanx, flanked by archers. Sometimes groups of archers were put at intervals along the line of armoured men. While the archers were effective at a distance, they were vulnerable to armoured infantry at close quarters and so they might fall back behind the men at arms when the enemy closed to hand to hand fighting. More heavily armoured archers, as was increasingly common by the later 15th century, would join the hand to hand fighting.

Many commanders sought to put their infantry into defensive positions of one sort or another. These might be behind field boundary hedges or ditches, inside villages or even specially dug fieldworks.

A new factor by the time of the Wars of the Roses was the advent of guns. These came in two forms: handguns and artillery. For the most part these made relatively little impact on tactical dispositions on the battlefield. Hand guns increased the death rate in the last few yards before the men got to work with hand weapons, while artillery increased the number of deaths at a distance. However, neither were so deadly as to alter the dispositions or tactical formations. The bigger guns rendered useless the old stone walled castles, one reason why sieges were relatively rare in the Wars of the Roses.

Although heavily armoured, mounted knights had fallen out of use there was still a role for horsemen. As noted above, Irish horsemen were sometimes hired to serve as scouts, but most commanders preferred to use Englishmen equipped as hobilars. These hobilars - also known as currours or prickers - were more lightly armed than knights and rode less expensive horses. Their roles were mostly off the battlefield. They scouted ahead and to the flanks of the army looking for the enemy. They rode ahead to secure bridges or fords. They rode off to carry messages to other commanders or to local authorities. They sought good campsites, bought - or in France stole - food supplies.

Even on the field of battle these hobilars had a use. They were kept in reserve to be unleashed on a fleeing enemy to use their speed to ride down fugitives. Or they could be thrown into action to disrupt a pursuit by enemy horsemen and so cover the retreat of the infantry. There were some occasions, admittedly rare, when hobilars performed a mounted charge. This tactic was rarely used as it was so rarely successful. Against formed infantry it was doomed to failure, but if they could catch infantry on the march or out of formation after crossing a stream then the hobilars could perform great service.

During the Wars of the Roses it was customary for an army to be divided into three "battles". Each battle consisted of a mix of soldier types, with archers and men at arms. The commander of the army usually took command of the central battle, with his more experienced subordinate leading the foreward battle and the third commander the rear battle. Any artillery present was usually kept with the central battle, as much for its commercial value as its use in fighting. Hobilars or other mounted troops would usually be formed outside this traditional structure. They would have their own commander answerable to the army commander, but would only rarely be actually with the army itself. More often the bulk of these men were off on detached duties of one kind or another, though rarely more than a day or two's ride from the army.

It was traditional for the central battle to be the largest, perhaps as strong as the other two put together. Some commanders preferred to vary this arrangement. The most usual variation was to increase the strength of the advance battle to make it capable of independent action. Some army commanders even preferred to put themselves in charge of the advance battle, delegating the central battle to the third in command.

It had become customary for English armies to be under the command of a nobleman - often the king or a prince of royal blood when campaigning in France. This was largely for political and social reasons. Nobles who had brought sizeable forces to the war could be relied upon to take orders from a social superior. However, senior nobles with great military talent were in short supply, so the English kings had got into the habit of appointing one or more highly experienced and skilful soldiers to be Constables to give advice to the nobleman in command. The exact nature of the relationship between the Constables and the noble commander is not known. Presumably there were times when the nobleman was only nominally in charge, with everyone present knowing that the Constable was the real man in charge. At other times a nobleman of talent would use his Constable more in the role of chief of staff to look after the more mundane organisational tasks of an army on the move.

In the context of the Wars of the Roses, armies tended to be commanded by the most politically important nobleman present. It tended to be these men who had called the army into existence and who decided what its purpose was to be. There were usually Constables present, and here their role seems to have been to offer advice when asked for it. They might be asked their opinion on any matter, but it was always up the nobleman in charge what decision to make. It was, in a very real sense, his head that was going to be on the block if anything went wrong.

Chapter 4
The Battle of Northampton

The Yorkist army marched north from London in heavy rain on 4 July. Warwick had decided to leave a quarter of his army in the city to keep an eye on a Lancastrian garrison in the Tower of London and to man the walls of London. The Earl of Salisbury, Lord Cobham and Sir John Wenlock commanded the London garrison. The artillery of the city was set up on Tower Hill and began firing at the Tower. The Yorkist artillery, meanwhile, was put on St Katherine's Wharf and likewise opened fire. The guns of the Tower, commanded by Lord Scale and Lord Hungerford, replied in kind.

The main army was, meanwhile, divided with one part heading towards Ely, where rumour had it the king was seeking refuge, and the other going towards Coventry where he had been known to be a week earlier. Two days later scouts

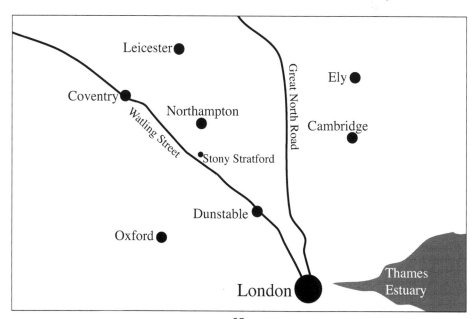

came in with the definite news that King Henry and a large army were camped at Northampton. The Yorkist army united at Dunstable and advanced up Watling Street (now the A5) as far as Stony Stratford before turning north up the road leading to Northampton.

At this point, the Yorkists decided to negotiate. They were in a delicate position, both politically and militarily. Their entire case rested on the claim that King Henry VI was surrounded by evil advisers who were both corrupt and dishonest. The Yorkists claimed to be loyal to the king, wanting merely to get rid of the wicked government and restore sound administration to England. But floating over the camp in front of them was the Royal Standard. King Henry VI himself was present, so any attack would be seen to be an attack on the king. Warwick, Edward and Fauconberg would have known very well that many, perhaps most, of their men were firmly loyal to the king and would not attack him. Not only

Delapre Abbey as it is today. The current buildings occupy the site of the medieval abbey but date to the 18th century.

36

The Eleanor Cross still stands where it was on the day of the battle, though it has been somewhat battered by the passing years. The cross was one of 12 such monuments erected by King Edward I to commemorate his wife, Queen Eleanor. The much loved queen died in Lincoln in 1290 and her embalmed body carried in procession to London for burial in Westminster Abbey. At every place where the body rested overnight, Edward ordered the erection of a great stone cross in memory of his beloved wife and queen. Of the original 12 only three remain, with that by Delapre Abbey being one of the best preserved. The Archbishop of Canterbury watched the battle from the steps of the cross, though the view across the battlefield is now blocked by the trees.

might the Yorkist army melt away if asked to commit treason, but the entire Yorkist movement might collapse. And that would almost certainly lead to the execution of York, Warwick and others.

Somehow Warwick had to find a way to portray himself as being in the right. Fortunately he had Archbishop Bouchier and a number of other bishops with him. Warwick now turned to them.

Warwick and Edward had in London already declared that all they wanted to do was lay their grievances before King Henry without their opponents being present. They would then happily submit to the royal decision confident that such a good and pious king as Henry would make the right decision. Now they repeated this message to Bouchier and asked him to deliver it to King Henry.

Mounting his horse, Bouchier and some half dozen other bishops rode on ahead of the Yorkist army to speak to the king. Bouchier and the bishops reached the Lancastrian camp on 9 July. What followed next was crucial. Bouchier was met by scouts and conducted to Delapre Abbey, where Henry, Buckingham and the other nobles were in residence while their army camped in the nearby deer park. Bouchier entered the dining hall and made for the king, but was intercepted by Buckingham who demanded to know what he wanted. Bouchier then repeated the message from Warwick that all he wanted was to speak to the king alone. Buckingham, of course, well knew Henry's fragile mental state and had no intention of allowing the smooth-tongued Warwick anywhere near him.

"The Earl of Warwick shall not come to the King's presence," said Buckingham, "and if he comes he shall die."

Bouchier again tried to speak to the king directly, but was stopped from doing so. He returned to his horse to take the message back to Warwick, but two of the bishops chose to stay with the king instead.

Bouchier met the Yorkist army towards evening as they were some six or so miles south of Northampton. He told Warwick, Edward and the other nobles what had taken place. Warwick put on a grave face and declared that it was as he feared. The evil advisers were in complete control of the king, so much that even the Archbishop of Canterbury had not been allowed to speak to the king directly. The only solution was a military one. No doubt Warwick and Edward made much of the fact that they were loyal to the king and had been rebuffed by Buckingham. Warwick ended by telling his supporters "At 2 o'clock tomorrow I will speak with the King or I will die".

On the morning of 10 July scouting hobilar cavalry were sent ahead to drive the Lancastrian scouts back into their camp. Riding with the hobilars was Warwick's herald, along with Lord Scrope and Lord Stafford. It was considered polite in medieval warfare for a final attempt to be made to find an amicable solution to even the most intransigent problem before blood was spilled. So while Scrope and Stafford sat on the ridge south of Delapre Abbey to put the arriving advance battle into formation, the herald trotted forward. Heralds traditionally enjoyed immunity in warfare to act as messengers and go-betweens. We do not know exactly what the herald shouted to Buckingham, but presumably it was another request to meet the king. Buckingham refused. The niceties over, the battle could begin.

Around noon Warwick, Edward and Fauconberg reached the ridge from which they could survey the enemy. What they saw cannot have filled them with much confidence.

The Lancastrians had rather fewer men than did the Yorkists. Contemporary

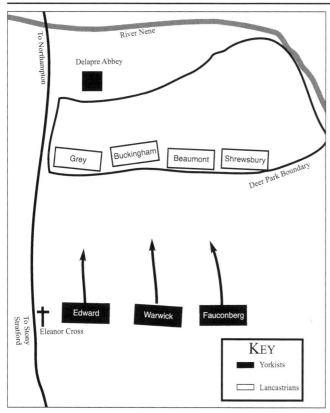

The battle opened a little after noon when the Yorkists advanced down off the ridge crowned by the Eleanor Cross to advance over open farmland toward the prepared defences of the Lancastrian army. A frontal advance was made necessary by the boggy nature of the riverside meadows after recent heavy rain.

accounts suggest Warwick had around 25,000 men and Buckingham some 20,000. Modern historians have reduced these figures to 8,000 and 5,000 respectively, but it is difficult to be certain of the truth.

But what the Lancastrians lost in numbers they gained in position. Buckingham had camped his men in a deer part belonging to Delapre Abbey, just south of the town of Northampton. The park was close to the main road north into Northampton with the River Nene to its north and boggy meadows to the east. The position could therefore be attacked only from the south or west, and the western approaches were probably almost as boggy as those to the east after the recent heavy rain. Warwick would therefore have to advance from the south.

The southern approaches to the deer park were covered in 1460 by open fields which, given the time of year, would probably have been filled with still-green grain crops. Wheat in the 15th century was taller than today, so the grain may have stood up to four feet tall. There were no hedges or trees to give cover. Warwick's men would need to advance across open ground swept by the archery of the defenders. To make the situation worse, Warwick could see more than a dozen pieces of artillery poking out from the enemy camp. Those guns would add their murderous fire to that of the archers.

Buckingham had had several days in Northampton and he had not wasted his time. The boundaries of the deer park were marked by a ditch about five feet deep, backed by a wooden fence some six feet or so tall. It was designed to keep deer in, not to keep men out, and by itself would not have been a terribly useful defensive work. However, Buckingham would seem to have demolished the fence and used the timbers to erect a defensive work on the inside of the ditch to make it a tough barrier for men seeking to get in.

These sorts of field works were not intended to be able to withstand a siege in the way a castle could, but to hinder the movement of troops on the battlefield. There were two key features needed by these works. First they had to provide shelter from incoming arrows. Given the power of bows at the time this meant that timber walls or fences had to be more than an inch thick. Secondly they had to be tall enough to stop a man scrambling over unassisted. Such a height might vary, but was generally taken to be around six feet. Anything under that and an attacker stood a chance of getting over the obstacle without too much difficulty.

Even in armour a man of the time would be able to manage such a fence. Such an obstacle would take up a lot of timber and take time to construct. More usually, therefore, an army would dig a ditch and place a timber wall on its lip so that the vertical distance from top of the wall to bottom of the ditch was greater than six feet. Buckingham had a ready made ditch in the deer park boundary, so his work had been speeded up. He would also seem, though this is not certain, to have added refinements in the form of sharpened stakes, pits in front of the ditch to trip the unwary and so forth. He certainly had dug elaborate emplacements for his artillery that gave them a fairly wide field of fire while the gunners were protected from in coming arrows.

Buckingham does not seem to have arranged his army in the traditional three battles, though he may have done. Each lord in his army led his own contingent. Buckingham himself took up a position beside the king's tent from where he could survey the entire camp boundary. He kept his own men close to him, presumably intending to lead them to any area of the defences that came under heavy pressure.

Scrope and Stafford had been arranging the arriving Yorkist army in traditional fashion. The advance guard under Fauconberg was put on the right of the ridge facing the enemy, perhaps with his right wing about where the modern golf club building is to be found. In the centre was the main battle commanded by the Earl of Warwick, positioned where Delapre Wood now flanks the northern edge of the modern A45 Northampton Bypass. On the left was the rear battle commanded by Edward, Earl of March. Its left wing rested on the main road beside Queen Eleanor's Cross. Bouchier and his clerics sat on the steps of the Cross. From there they could see the Lancastrian camp, but felt safe as men of the Church under the shadow of a sacred monument.

In the pause that followed, Warwick rode along the line of his army. At intervals he stopped to make an identical speech to his men, so that everyone heard it. He repeated the familiar story about evil advisers. He told his men that his quarrel was with those advisers only, not with King Henry nor with the soldiers in the enemy camp, who had simply been led astray. Pointing to the banner fluttering

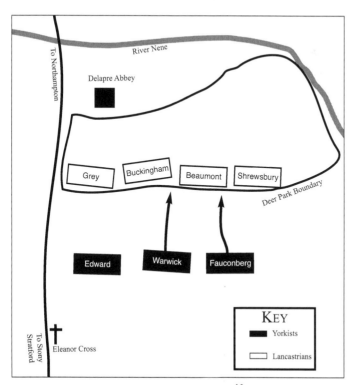

As Warwick and Fauconberg charged the Lancastrian defences, the rear guard commanded by Edward hung back and deluged the Lancastrian defences with volley after volley of arrow shots.

over the enemy camp, Warwick then named the men he wanted dead or captured: The Duke of Buckingham, the Earl of Shrewsbury, Lord Egremont and Lord Beaumont. As he finished a sudden heavy shower of rain lashed across the landscape.

Then the trumpets sounded and the Yorkist army began to advance. They walked down the slope, heading north across the open grain fields that are now covered by the Delapre Golf Course. As they neared the enemy camp arrows began to fly. Shooting while standing still behind defences, the Lancastrians could take better aim, shoot more quickly and were protected from enemy shots. The Yorkists were in the open and on the move. Their archers stopped now and then to shoot, but then trotted forwards to keep up with the men at arms and billmen. Undoubtedly the Yorkists got the worse of this exchange.

On the left wing, however, something odd was happening. Edward had stopped his battle from advancing. While Warwick and Fauconberg kept going, Edward stopped and had his archers shoot continuously. It was an unusual tactic, but one seemingly designed to force the Lancastrians to keep their heads down while Warwick and Fauconberg rushed across the last tens of yards to the defended deer park.

One weapon that was notable by its silence was the artillery of the Lancastrians. The sudden shower of rain had come at the worst possible moment for the gunners. They had their barrels of recently mixed gunpowder open and their cloth bags of pre-weighed powder charges lined up ready to load. The rain had drenched the lot and rendered it useless. After a few desultory shots that did no damage at all the guns fell silent. It would be hours before more powder would be ready, and by then the battle would be over.

Warwick and Fauconberg's men surged forward at the field defences. While archers held back and shot at the enemy, armoured men scrambled down into the muddy ditch, then tried to get up the other side and over the wooden fence. Time and again they attacked, time and again they were thrown back. The ditch was filling with bodies as the dead and wounded slithered back down from the Lancastrian defences. For perhaps twenty minutes the fighting went on without respite.

Then Edward ordered his archers to cease shooting and formed his armoured infantry up to attack. But first he made a short speech. He pointed to a banner on the right flank of the Lancastrian position. It bore a black ragged staff on a green field. Edward told his men to attack toward that banner, but that no man who had

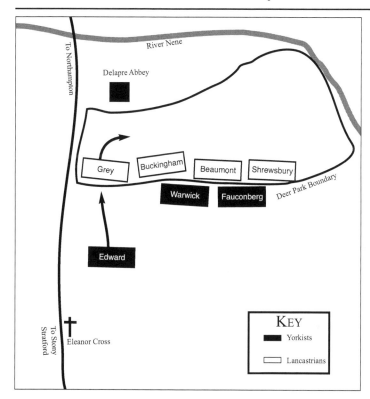

The battle reached its climax about 1.15pm as Edward's division got into the fortified deer park with the assistance of the turncoat Lord Grey.

the badge of a black staff on a green field sewn to his chest was to be harmed. Those men, Edward said, were Yorkists. And so it proved to be.

As Edward led his men at the defences they were met not by arrows or blades, but by helpful hands that pulled them up and over. The black staff was the badge of Lord Edmund Grey of Ruthin. Warwick had been in touch with Grey during the advance from London and had promised him the disputed manor of Ampthill if he changed sides. Grey had agreed. Now the deal bore fruit.

Edward had his men inside the Lancastrian defences. Pausing to get his men in formation he led them at the charge to take the defenders in flank and rear. The Lancastrian defence collapsed. With enemies in front, behind and on the flank, the Lancastrian soldiers broke and fled. Now what had been a strong defensive position became a deathtrap. The river was to their north and east, and most of the men were weighed down by heavy armour. Some tried to strip off their armour, others did not. How many were drowned was never properly discovered.

Buckingham did not attempt to flee. He stood his ground and went down fighting valiantly. The Earl of Shrewsbury also died, so did Beaumont and Egremont. Lord Stafford spotted a Lancastrian knight with whom he had a personal grudge. Sir William Lucy had married in an arranged marriage Stafford's sweetheart. A swift sword thrust rendered Lady Lucy a widow, and a few weeks later she became Lady Stafford. As the rout developed into a potential bloodbath, Warwick began shouting to his men to show mercy. He wanted the leaders dead, not the followers. A Yorkist archer named Henry Montfort wrestled a knight to the ground hoping to extract a ransom from his prisoner, only to find that the knight was King Henry himself.

The hapless King Henry was led to where Warwick was trying to rally some of his men to guard against a surprise counterattack should the Lancastrians prove capable of such a thing. Recognising the king, Warwick flung himself to his knees, thanked God for the king's safety and declared his undying loyalty to Henry. It was, as Warwick had predicted, not yet 2 o'clock.

Warwick sent King Henry under guard into the Abbey to rest and be fed. As

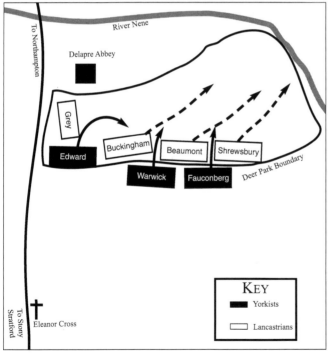

Soon after Edward broke into the fortified deer park he led his men to attack Buckingham's men in the flank and rear. The Lancastrians then broke and fled, though they were to find their escape route blocked by the River Nene.

soon as the fighting was over, Warwick and Edward escorted the King off the battlefield and into Northampton town. The procession was carried out with all due formality. Warwick himself, as the senior noble present, walked backwards in front of the king carrying the sword of state upright. A banquet was ordered and court ceremonial followed carefully to emphasise the loyalty of Warwick and Edward to the king.

Fauconberg was left on the battlefield to clear up. He counted 300 Lancastrian bodies, and around 100 Yorkists. The heralds moved around the battlefield to identify knights, nobles and men of rank among the dead. The bodies of those who were thought to have relatives who might care were put to one side. Their possessions were gathered up and messages written to the distant relatives asking for instructions. The bodies of the common soldiers were left to their comrades. Possessions and arms were collected up to be taken home. The enemy were simply stripped of anything useful. The bodies were then given Christian burial in the grounds of the Abbey.

The battle was over.

A view across the battlefield today. The Yorkists advanced down the slope on the left as they headed north to attack the fortifications to the right of this picture. The lake seen here was caused by flooding after heavy rain.

CHAPTER 5
AFTERMATH

For three days after the Battle of Northampton, Warwick and Edward remained in the town with King Henry. Horsemen were sent out in all directions seeking fugitive Lancastrians or the approach of a fresh enemy army, while messengers were sent to carry news of the battle to London, and to the Duke of York in Ireland. Having satisfied themselves that there was no immediate threat, the Yorkists marched back to London.

When they reached the capital they found that word of their victory had been sent to the Tower. Lord Scales and Lord Hungerford were now seeking terms of surrender. Warwick replied that the defenders could go free, or remain in the King's service as they wished, so long as they surrendered at once and did no damage to the Tower or its contents. Hungerford promptly opened the gates and hauled down his flag. After some questioning by Warwick, he left London for his estates. Scales, however, did not trust Warwick and chose to flee in a rowing boat going upstream to seek sanctuary at Westminster Abbey. He was spotted by a group of Thames boatmen who gave chase in their boats, overhauled the hapless lord and killed him. His body was later given a dignified burial on the orders of Edward. Warwick began acting in the king's name, taking control of government pending the arrival of the Duke of York.

Queen Margaret heard the news of Northampton at Coventry. The citizens of the town, and even some of her servants, turned on her. She was robbed of all her possessions and thrown out. Accompanied only by her young son and a 14 year old servant, Margaret walked to Wales where she took ship to Scotland to seek sanctuary and help.

The Yorkist cause appeared to be triumphant. The Duke of York landed in Chester and marched southeast towards London. Warwick had summoned a Parliament to meet at Westminster on 10 October and it was widely reported that the main business would be to appoint a new Regency Council with York again as Protector. Lords favouring York hurried to London, those opposing him stayed away. The towns and counties similarly took care to send men to Parliament who either favoured York, or at least did not openly oppose him.

On the morning of 10 October the Parliament met with Warwick presiding. The opening formalities were concluded and some speeches made. Then trumpets were heard outside and the tramping boots of armed men echoed through the windows. The doors of the Great Hall of Westminster were ceremoniously opened and in strode the Duke of York. There were gasps of astonishment. His trumpeters and heralds did not wear the arms and badges of York, but of the King of England. And in front of York walked a man carrying the Sword of State that could be carried only in front of the King of England.

York strode across the hall and walked up to the throne. He put his hand on the cushion, as did the king before taking his seat to preside over Parliament. York turned for it was at this moment that tradition demanded that the assembled men and lords of Parliament bowed to the king. He was met instead by a sea of grim faces, and not a single man bowed - not even Warwick who seems to have

The murder of the youthful Earl of Rutland a few months after the Battle of Northampton followed the death of his father the Duke of York at the Battle of Wakefield.

been taken as much by surprise as everyone else. After several seconds of tense silence, Archbishop Bouchier hesitantly edged forwards. He bowed slightly to York and asked "Has your grace perhaps come to visit the king?"

York exploded in fury and stormed out.

Later that day lawyers acting for York arrived at Parliament to present a Bill that would have dethroned Henry and made York king. The Bill argued that York was the true heir to the throne from King Edward III, that Henry VI was the grandson of the usurper Henry IV and therefore was no true king. In legal terms, York may have been correct. But in political terms he was very badly wrong.

While the lawyers argued, lords and men slipped away from London as quietly as they could manage. Warwick noticed them go, and began to get worried. York would have none of it.

Told that Queen Margaret had crossed the border from Scotland with a small band of mercenaries, York marched north to defeat her. When he got to Wakefield in Yorkshire he found that Margaret's army had been swelled by large numbers of lords and men who opposed York's grab for the throne. York was killed in the ensuing battle and his son, the Earl of Rutland, was murdered as he tried to escape.

York's death solved nothing. The Wars of the Roses would continue.

ALSO AVAILABLE IN THIS SERIES

The Battle of Wimbledon 568
The Battle of Lincoln 1141
The Battle of Chesterfield 1266
The Battle of Northampton 1460
The Battle of Losecoat Field 1470
The Sieges of Newark 1643-46
The Siege of Leicester 1645
More to come